WARS DAY BY DAY

WORLD WAR II

1939–1945

Hermann Black

BROWN
BEAR
BOOKS

Published by Brown Bear Books Limited
An imprint of
The Brown Reference Group plc
68 Topstone Road
Redding
Connecticut
06896
USA
www.brownreference.com

This hardcover edition is distributed in the United States by:
Black Rabbit Books
P.O. Box 3263
Mankato, MN 56002

ISBN: 978-1-933834-41-2

Library of Congress Cataloging-in-Publication Data

Black, Hermann.
  World War II / Hermann Black.
     p. cm. -- (Wars day by day)
  Summary: "In a time line format, describes the causes leading up to World War II and political events and battles during the war. Includes primary source quotes"--Provided by publisher.
  Includes bibliographical references and index.
  ISBN 978-1-933834-41-2
  1. World War, 1939-1945--Chronology--Juvenile literature. I. Title. II. Title: World War Two. III. Title: World War 2. IV. Series.

D743.7.B57 2009
940.53--dc22

                                                                    2007050003

Designer: Reg Cox
Creative Director: Jeni Child
Children's Publisher: Anne O'Daly
Editorial Director: Lindsey Lowe
Design Manager: Sarah Williams
Editor: Peter Darman

Printed and bound in the United States

Contents

Introduction

At the end of World War I in November 1918 Germany had been defeated. The Treaty of Versailles drawn up by the victors—Britain, France, and the United States—was intended to prevent any future war in Europe. It cut Germany's army to 100,000 men and imposed huge fines on the Germans to compensate for the damage done during World War I. These payments were called reparations.

Germany had little money after the war. This meant it fell behind in its reparations payments. As punishment, France took over a part of Germany called the Ruhr, which was a key industrial center. This caused a collapse of the German economy. Millions of Germans lost their jobs. The price of goods and food increased so quickly that many people could not afford enough food to eat. The German currency became worthless. In 1929 a worldwide economic collapse began, which left millions of Germans jobless. Many Germans were angry and confused. They blamed the Treaty of Versailles for many of their problems.

In such an atmosphere, many Germans were attracted to the extreme views of a former

In the 1930s, Hitler's Germany took over foreign lands that contained German-speaking peoples—the Sudetenland and Austria. Germany tried to take Polish land as well, which caused World War II.

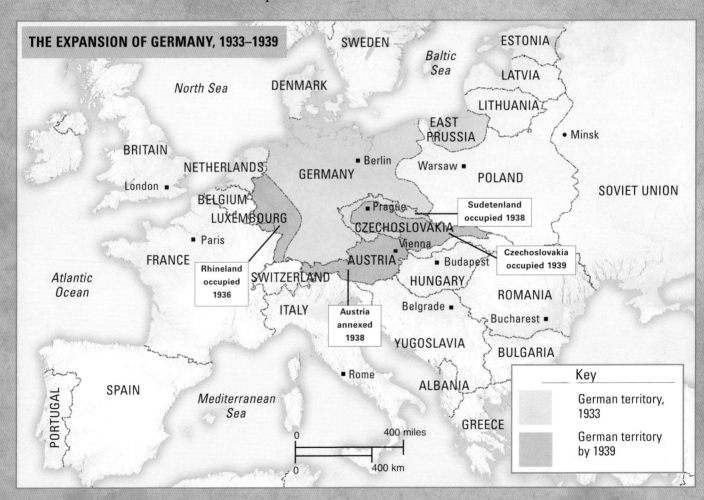

THE EXPANSION OF GERMANY, 1933–1939

SWEDEN
Baltic Sea
ESTONIA
LATVIA
LITHUANIA
North Sea
DENMARK
EAST PRUSSIA
• Minsk
BRITAIN
NETHERLANDS
GERMANY
• Berlin
Warsaw •
POLAND
SOVIET UNION
London •
BELGIUM
LUXEMBOURG
• Prague
Sudetenland occupied 1938
CZECHOSLOVAKIA
• Paris
• Vienna
Czechoslovakia occupied 1939
FRANCE
Rhineland occupied 1936
SWITZERLAND
AUSTRIA
• Budapest
HUNGARY
Atlantic Ocean
ITALY
Austria annexed 1938
Belgrade •
ROMANIA
• Bucharest
YUGOSLAVIA
BULGARIA
• Rome
ALBANIA
GREECE
PORTUGAL
SPAIN
Mediterranean Sea

0   400 miles

0   400 km

Key

German territory, 1933

German territory by 1939

soldier named Adolf Hitler. Hitler's National Socialist German Workers' Party, or Nazi Party, blamed Germany's crisis on communists and Jews. So many people agreed with him that in 1933 Hitler became Germany's chancellor. Once in power, he created new jobs and built up the armed forces. This made him popular. But he also became a dictator, and persecuted Jews and communists.

The Treaty of Versailles had created new countries in Europe, such as Czechoslovakia. Many German-speaking people lived in these countries. Hitler was determined to make them citizens of Germany. He did this by taking over Czechoslovakia and Austria in the 1930s.

Italy and Japan

To the south, Italy had been ruled by the dictator Benito Mussolini since 1922. He also built up his country's armed forces and glorified war. It was natural, therefore, that Germany and Italy should become allies in the 1930s.

In East Asia, Japan had been on the winning side in World War I. However, Japan had had to give up Chinese lands it had conquered in an earlier war with Russia. The Japanese resented the fact that Britain and the United States treated them like a second-class nation. The Japanese also resented the fact that they had to buy nearly all their food, metal, and oil from abroad. Like the European nations, they wanted colonies in the Far East that could provide these goods.

In the 1920s and 1930s Japan was determined to have an empire of its own to be a "great power." And it also needed raw materials such as oil and metal, to keep the navy running and build new weapons for the army. Japan attacked China in the 1930s. But Japan wanted more land and oil. This led to attacks on Britain and the United States in 1941.

Japan invaded Manchuria (a northern province of China) in 1931, and in 1937 invaded the rest of China. This was condemned by the League of Nations. The League was made up of many nations, but was led by Britain and France (the United States was not a member). The League criticized Germany, Italy, and Japan for their aggression in the 1930s. But they ignored the League and formed their own alliance called the Rome-Berlin-Tokyo Axis. They were known as the Axis nations.

Hitler started threatening Poland about German lands that had passed to the Poles (land between Germany and East Prussia called the "Polish Corridor"). Britain and France agreed to defend Poland against Germany. Hitler ignored them and attacked Poland on September 1, 1939. World War II had begun.

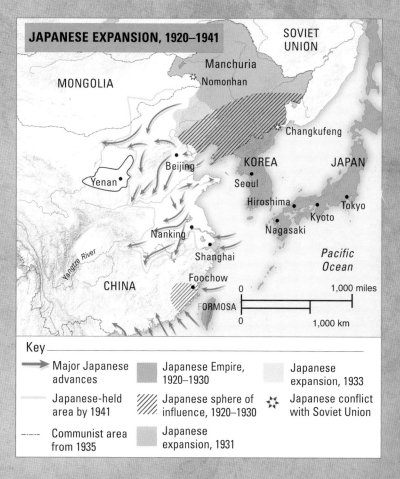

JAPANESE EXPANSION, 1920–1941

Key

→ Major Japanese advances

Japanese-held area by 1941

----- Communist area from 1935

Japanese Empire, 1920–1930

//// Japanese sphere of influence, 1920–1930

Japanese expansion, 1931

Japanese expansion, 1933

Japanese conflict with Soviet Union

JANUARY 18, 1919, France

The leaders of the victorious nations of World War I gather in Paris to talk about a treaty with the defeated countries of Germany and Austria-Hungary. These leaders include President Woodrow Wilson of the United States, British Prime Minister Lloyd George, French Prime Minister Georges Clemenceau, and the prime minister of Italy, Vittorio Emanuele Orlando.

JANUARY 21, 1919, Ireland

Sinn Fein ("Ourselves Alone"), an Irish group that wants Ireland to be free from British rule, declares Ireland independent. This sparks a rebellion against the British. The British send 100,000 troops and paramilitaries (part-time soldiers) to Ireland to crush the revolt.

APRIL 13, 1919, India

In India, former lawyer Mahatma Gandhi is leading a campaign to free the country from British rule. A large crowd of Gandhi supporters gathers at Amritsar in the Punjab. British troops commanded by General Reginald Dyer open fire on the unarmed crowd, killing 379 people and wounding 1,208. The British authorities do not punish Dyer, which causes outrage throughout India.

Communist "Red" Russian troops marching to fight "White" forces.

JUNE 28, 1919, France

The treaty produced at the talks in Paris is signed in the Hall of Mirrors at the Palace of Versailles. The Treaty of Versailles blames Germany for starting World War I and orders it to pay a huge fine.

JULY 21, 1919, Britain

German sailors deliberately sink, or scuttle, their ships at Scapa Flow in Britain's Orkney Islands. This is to stop the British making use of the German High Seas Fleet.

SEPTEMBER 2, 1919, Russia

In Russia, a civil war is raging between the "Reds" (communists) and the "Whites" (monarchists). The "Whites" capture the

EYEWITNESS: Winston Churchill on the Amritsar Massacre, July 1920

"Unrest in India erupted into open violence. In April 1919, under the orders of General Dyer, troops opened fire on a crowd at Amritsar, killing 379 unarmed civilians and wounding over a thousand. The Commander-in-Chief in India recommended that General Dyer should be ordered to retire, and the matter came before the Army Council for review. The Council accepted the recommendation, as did the Cabinet."

Civil war – a war between opposing groups of citizens of the same country.

Ukrainian city of Kiev. Other "White" troops under Peter Wrangel capture Tsaritsin (later Stalingrad) on June 17, but are forced to retreat.

AUGUST 16–25, 1920, Poland
Polish troops attack "Red" Russian armies near Warsaw. The Poles smash through the Russian center, forcing the "Reds" to retreat. Russian casualties total 150,000 men.

NOVEMBER 14, 1920, Russia
British warships evacuate Peter Wrangel's "White" forces from the Crimea. The evacuation marks the end of the Russian Civil War and a "Red" victory.

NOVEMBER 12, 1921, United States
The leading powers meet in Washington, D.C., to sign treaties aimed to prevent future wars. The Four-Power Act, signed on December 13, agrees that Britain, France, Japan, and the United States will peacefully solve any rival claims to land in the Pacific Ocean.

Italian fascist leader Benito Mussolini (second from right) in 1922.

OCTOBER 28, 1922, Italy
Fascist leader Benito Mussolini leads his followers, called "Blackshirts," in the "March on Rome." He forces the government and king to give him complete power as a dictator. He begins a reign of terror against his opponents.

TURNING POINTS: The Treaty of Versailles

Versailles was a shock to the German delegation (seen at right). Germany lost a tenth of its territory and population to France in the west and Poland in the east. The losses included the "Polish Corridor." This slice of territory gave Poland access to the Baltic Sea. Germany also had to accept the blame for starting World War I. The Germans had to pay a huge fine for the damage suffered by the victors. Finally, the mighty German Army was cut to 100,000 men.

Fascist – a supporter of a strongly nationalistic and militaristic political party.

TURNING POINTS: Extreme politics

Fascism and communism were extreme forms of right- and left-wing politics, respectively. Both were popular in the 1920s and 1930s in Europe. Germany (at right) and Italy both had fascist leaders. They tried to make their countries strong by raising large armies and conquering other states. Russia was a communist country. It was prepared to use war to spread communism to other countries. Both fascism and communism turned people into slaves. Neither system allowed individuals any freedom.

NOVEMBER 9, 1923, Germany
Adolf Hitler leads the right-wing National Socialist German Workers' Party (Nazi Party) in an anti-government revolt in Munich. It fails. Hitler is sent to prison for five years, but serves only nine months.

MARCH 26, 1926, China
In China's civil war, Nationalist forces under General Chiang Kai-shek capture the city of Nanking. The Nationalists are trying to defeat the warlords and communists.

Armed members of Adolf Hitler's Nazi Party wearing swastika armbands.

JULY 28, 1930, China
Communist forces capture Chang-sha in central China, but the Nationalists retake the city. They begin "bandit suppression" campaigns against the communists.

JANUARY 30, 1933, Germany
Nazi leader Adolf Hitler becomes chancellor (leader) of Germany following elections.

JUNE 30, 1934, Germany
More than 70 members of the Nazi Party are murdered on Adolf Hitler's orders. Hitler believes they are a threat to his absolute authority. The event is known as "the Night of the Long Knives."

OCTOBER 3, 1935, Ethiopia
Italian troops invade Ethiopia in eastern Africa. The surprise attack is part of Benito Mussolini's plan to create an Italian empire in Africa.

Warlord – a military commander who has political power over a region.

EYEWITNESS: Noel Monks, British journalist, on the bombing of Guernica

"I was the first correspondent to reach Guernica, and was immediately pressed into service by some Basque soldiers collecting charred bodies that the flames had passed over. Some of the soldiers were sobbing like children. There were flames and smoke and grit. Houses were collapsing into the inferno. The only things left standing were a church, a sacred tree, and, just outside the town, a small munitions factory."

AUGUST 15, 1936, Spain
The Spanish Civil War begins when troops in Spain and in Spanish Morocco rebel against Manuel Azãna's Republican government. General Francisco Franco leads the rebels, who become known as Nationalists.

APRIL 25, 1937, Spain
German aircraft, part of the Condor Legion that is fighting on the side of the Nationalists, bomb the town of Guernica. Some 1,600 civilians are killed and nearly 900 wounded.

JULY 7, 1937, China
Japanese troops attack Chinese units at the Marco Polo Bridge near Beijing. The attack is part of Japan's plan to take over China and get access to its resources.

MARCH 12, 1938, Germany
Hitler orders the German takeover of Austria, where some six million Germans live. Many Austrians welcome the move, which is completed the next day. Italian leader Benito Mussolini also supports German *Anschluss* ("Union") with Austria.

JULY 11, 1938, China
Fighting breaks out between the Soviet Union and Japan, which is occupying Manchuria and Korea. The Soviets beat off the Japanese attacks by mid-August.

SEPTEMBER 29, 1938, Germany
Adolf Hitler meets Italian leader Benito Mussolini, British Prime Minister Neville Chamberlain, and Edouard Daladier, France's prime minister, at Munich. Hitler wants to take over Czechoslovakia, where many Germans live. Britain and France agree to his demands, believing that this will bring peace. The Sudetenland region of Czechoslovakia becomes part of Germany.

Nationalist field guns prepare to fire in the Spanish Civil War.

Rebel – someone who fights against a government or leader.

NOVEMBER 9–10, 1938, Germany

Nazis attack German Jews and their property, particularly synagogues. The attacks become known as *Kristallnacht* ("Crystal Night") because of the glass from smashed windows that litters the roads and sidewalks. People outside Germany—and many Germans—are horrified.

JANUARY 26, 1939, Spain

Nationalists capture Barcelona, the Republican-held capital of Catalonia.

MARCH 10, 1939, Czechoslovakia

Adolf Hitler begins the takeover of Bohemia and Moravia, parts of Czechoslovakia where many Germans live. The operation is completed by March 16. Czechoslovakia ceases to exist.

MARCH 28, 1939, Spain

Nationalist troops enter the capital, Madrid. They have won the civil war. The civil war

A synagogue burns following the Nazi attacks on "Crystal Night."

has cost the lives of some 300,000 Spaniards. Nationalist leader General Francisco Franco is now ruler of Spain.

MAY 22, 1939, Italy

The government agrees closer military ties with Germany. The stronger alliance

TURNING POINTS: Appeasement

Appeasement began in the early 1930s in Britain and France. Politicians such as British leader Neville Chamberlain (at left of picture) and French minister Édouard Daladier thought that Adolf Hitler's demands for the return of "German" areas were fair. They argued that if they gave in to Hitler he would not go to war. But Hitler saw their attitude as proof that Britain and France were weak. It convinced him that if he went to war they would not interfere.

Appeasement – avoiding conflict by giving in to someone's demands.

EYEWITNESS: K.S. Karol, Polish cadet, September 1939

"The smell along the road was unchanginig. It was the smell of dead horses that no one had bothered to bury and that stank to high heaven. We moved only at night and we learned to sleep while marching; smoking was forbidden out of fear that the glow off a cigarette could bring down on us the all-powerful Luftwaffe. But along the roads, day or night, we were never alone; other soldiers and civilians were also marching."

between the two countries becomes known as the "Pact of Steel."

AUGUST 23 Germany

Germany signs a nonaggression pact with the Soviet Union. The Soviets agree not to oppose a German invasion of Poland. In return, they and the Germans will divide Poland between them.

SEPTEMBER 1 Poland

A German force of 53 divisions, supported by 1,600 aircraft, invades Poland. Poland has few tanks and aircraft. The Poles are quickly overwhelmed.

SEPTEMBER 2 Britain and France

Britain and France both threaten war if Germany does not withdraw immediately from Poland. The Germans ignore the demands.

SEPTEMBER 3 Britain and France

Britain, France, Australia, and New Zealand declare war on Nazi Germany.

SEPTEMBER 3 Atlantic Ocean

The German submarine *U-30* mistakes the British liner *Athenia* for a warship. The submarine sinks the ship. Some 112 civilian passengers drown.

SEPTEMBER 6 Poland

The Polish government and high command flee Warsaw. They order Polish forces to withdraw to the south of the country. Nazi troops advance to Lódz, near Warsaw, and capture Cracow.

German troops tear down a border post as they advance into Poland.

Division – an army unit made up of 15,000 to 20,000 soldiers.

SEPTEMBER 8 Poland

The German Tenth Army reaches the outskirts of Warsaw, the capital. Elsewhere, the German Fourteenth Army reaches Przemysl. General Heinz Guderian's *panzer* (tank) units advance east of Warsaw as far as the Bug River.

SEPTEMBER 9 Poland

The Poles launch a counterattack against the German Eighth Army to the south of Warsaw. The attack over the Bzura River is initially a success. But then the Germans counterattack and are able to push back the Polish troops.

SEPTEMBER 10 France

Troops of the British Expeditionary Force (BEF) begin to land in France to help the French fight the Germans. Some 160,000 men and 24,000 vehicles arrive during the course of September.

The British aircraft carrier *Courageous*, which was sunk by a U-boat in 1939.

SEPTEMBER 17 Atlantic Ocean

The British aircraft carrier HMS *Courageous* is sunk by the German submarine *U-29*. The aircraft carrier *Ark Royal* has escaped a similar submarine attack just three days earlier. The naval high command orders Britain's aircraft carriers into port to save them from being sunk.

KEY PEOPLE: Adolf Hitler

Adolf Hitler (1889–1945) was the German leader of the Nazi Party. He thought that Germany's economic problems could be overcome by the conquest of other lands and by expelling Jews and other groups from Germany. Hitler was elected chancellor in 1933 and made himself *Führer*, or supreme leader, of the Third Reich. Hitler began World War II when he invaded Poland in 1939. Facing defeat in 1945, he took his own life.

Expeditionary force – an army sent to serve abroad.

EYEWITNESS: Mollie Panter-Downes, London 1939

"Gas masks have suddenly become part of everyday civilian equipment and everybody is carrying the square cardboard cartons that look as though they might contain a pound of grapes for a sick friend. Admirals stump jauntily up Whitehall with their gas masks slung neatly in knapsacks over their shoulders. Last night London was completely blacked out."

SEPTEMBER 17–30 Poland
Under the terms of a secret clause in the 1939 pact with Germany, the Soviet Red Army invades Poland. It meets little resistance on Poland's eastern border: The Polish Army is fighting for its life in the west.

SEPTEMBER 18–30 Poland
Poland is defeated. The Polish government and high command flee to Romania, where they are imprisoned. A government-in-exile is formed and many Poles escape to Britain and France. Poland is split into two zones of occupation, one German, one Russian. Germany has lost 10,572 troops and the Soviet Union has lost 734 men killed in the campaign. Around 50,000 Poles are killed and 750,000 captured.

SEPTEMBER 27 Germany
Adolf Hitler tells his senior generals of his plans for an attack against France, Belgium, and Holland. The attack will take place this year. The generals object to Hitler making plans without their knowledge. They argue that Germany is not ready to launch such an attack. In the event, the attack is constantly delayed due to bad weather.

SEPTEMBER 29 USSR
After occupying Poland, the Soviet Union aims to extend its control over the Baltic coast. It hopes to reduce the chance of any German threat. During the next few weeks the Soviets gain bases and sign "mutual assistance" agreements with Lithuania, Latvia, and Estonia. Finland, however, will not agree to Soviet demands. It prepares its army to meet a Soviet attack.

Defeated Polish troops give themselves up to a German officer (left).

Occupation – military control of part of a country by forces from another.

EYEWITNESS: Leland Stowe, Oslo, April 9, 1940

"Less than fifteen hundred German soldiers had occupied Norway's capital while thousands of dazed, bewildered citizens looked dumbly on. Not a bomb had been dropped inside Oslo. This handful of troops had arrived by air, since daybreak that morning. They had only small weapons—but absolutely incredible discipline and nerve. They were an amazingly tiny band of men, but they marched in like conquerors. They were."

OCTOBER 14 North Sea
The battleship HMS *Royal Oak* is sunk in the British base at Scapa Flow in the Orkney Islands. The U-boat attack costs 786 lives. Defenses at the base are improved.

NOVEMBER 30 Finland
A Soviet force of more than 600,000 men attacks Finland. Soviet aircraft bomb the capital, Helsinki. Field Marshal Karl von Mannerheim leads Finland's defense with a force consisting mainly of reservists. The Finns are inferior in numbers and weapons to the Soviets, but the main Soviet attack is held at the Mannerheim Line. This system of defenses was built during World War I (1914–18) through rugged terrain and forest. As the war progresses, Finnish ski troops launch hit-and-run raids on Red Army troops, who are struggling because they have no winter clothing.

DECEMBER 2 Finland
The League of Nations tries to stop the war in Finland. The Soviet Union is a member of the League, but rejects its involvement. The League expels the Soviets on December 14.

DECEMBER 16 Finland
After advancing to the Mannerheim Line, the Soviets attack again. The Finns have few tanks and little artillery. They use home-made "Molotov Cocktails" (bottles filled with gasoline) to destroy enemy tanks.

The German pocket battleship *Graf Spee* burns before it is scuttled.

DECEMBER 13 Atlantic Ocean
In the Battle of the River Plate, British warships fight the German pocket battleship *Graf Spee* at the mouth of the Plate River, off Uruguay. The British vessels are damaged, but the *Graf Spee* is forced to withdraw to neutral Uruguay for repairs. British ships trap it in port. The *Graf Spee* is scuttled (sunk) by its crew on December 17.

Reservists – part of an army called on to fight in an emergency.

FEBRUARY 16, 1940, Norway
The British destroyer HMS *Cossack* enters neutral waters off Norway to rescue 299 British merchant sailors held on the German transport *Altmark*.

MARCH 11 Soviet Union
Finland and the Soviet Union agree a treaty to end the war between them. Finland loses 10 percent of its territory to the Soviets. War losses are 200,000 Soviet troops and 25,000 Finns.

German troops arrive in Oslo, capital of Norway, in April 1940.

APRIL 9 Norway and Denmark
A German invasion force, including warships and 1,000 aircraft, attacks Denmark and Norway. Denmark is overrun immediately. Although Norwegian forces resist, they have no tanks and little artillery. Their coastal defenses and navy are also very poor.

APRIL 14–19 Norway
More than 10,000 Allied troops land to help the Norwegians fight the Germans.

MAY 7–10 Britain
Prime Minister Neville Chamberlain resigns. Winston Churchill replaces him.

TURNING POINTS: *Blitzkrieg*

Blitzkrieg is a German term meaning "lightning war." It was a military tactic that aimed to defeat an enemy by a single, fast attack. *Blitzkrieg* required many tanks (at right), mobile artillery, and aircraft. *Blitzkrieg* always avoided enemy strongpoints. Instead, it targeted enemy rear areas where supplies were located. German infantry surrounded enemy troops and forced them to surrender. German planes destroyed most enemy aircraft on the ground in the war's first few days.

Pocket battleship – a powerful warship smaller than a battleship.

German vehicles make rapid progress during the Battle of France.

MAY 12–14 France

German tanks smash through the forested Ardennes region in eastern France and advance west. They open a 50-mile (75-km) gap in the Allied frontline. This drives a wedge between the Allied armies in France and those in Belgium.

MAY 26 France

Operation Dynamo begins to evacuate Allied forces who have retreated to the port of Dunkirk. An assorted fleet of pleasure boats, commercial craft, and naval vessels crosses and recrosses the English Channel to rescue the troops from the beaches.

MAY 28 Belgium

King Leopold of Belgium surrenders. His forces are surrounded after the Allied withdrawal to Dunkirk.

MAY 31 United States

President Franklin D. Roosevelt launches a huge arms-building "defense program."

MAY 10 Holland and Belgium

Nazi paratroopers seize Belgium's key frontier fortress, Eben Emael, and land in Holland. British and French armies advance into Belgium to meet what they think is the main German assault. However, the main German attack will take place to the south, in the Ardennes.

KEY PEOPLE: Winston Churchill

Winston Spencer Churchill (1874–1965) was one of World War II's major personalities. He was a former soldier, journalist, and politician who became British prime minister in 1940. The Nazis seemed close to victory, but he helped turn British fortunes around. He dismissed any sign of defeatism and rallied the nation to keep fighting. Churchill also made strong alliances with the United States and appointed fine generals to run the war.

Evacuation – the removal of people from a dangerous area.

EYEWITNESS: General Erwin Rommel, France, May 1940

"The tanks now rolled in a long column through the line of fortifications and on towards the first houses, which had been set alight by our fire. In the moonlight we could see the men of 7th Motorcycle Battalion moving forward on foot beside us. Occasionally an enemy machine-gun or anti-tank gun fired, but none of their shots came anywhere near us. Our artillery was dropping heavy fire on villages and the road."

JUNE 4–9 Norway
British and French troops begin to leave Norway. King Haakon and the government leave for Britain on the 7th. The king orders Norwegian forces to stop fighting on June 9, after losing 1,335 men in the war. Total Allied losses are 5,600. German losses total 3,692 men.

JUNE 3–4 France
Operation Dynamo ends. The "little ships" have rescued 338,226 men—two-thirds of them British—from the beaches of Dunkirk.

JUNE 5–12 France
The Germans launch Operation Red, a drive toward the capital, Paris. Some French troops fight bravely, but many units lack men, supplies, and guns. The French begin to withdraw south. Their morale crumbles.

JUNE 10 Italy
Italy declares war on France and Britain. Benito Mussolini, Italy's fascist leader, is eager to take advantage of France's collapse. Canada declares war on Italy on the 10th; Australia, New Zealand, and South Africa follow the next day.

JUNE 14 France
The French declare Paris an "open city"—meaning that they will not defend it—in order to save it from destruction. German troops enter the city unopposed.

JUNE 16–24 France
New prime minister Marshal Henri-Philippe Pétain takes power and promises to request a peace treaty with Germany. The treaty leaves Germany in control of two-thirds of France, including the Channel and Atlantic coasts. The south, now known as Vichy France, will be under French rule. French casualties since May 10 are 85,000, British 3,475, and German 27,074.

Italian three-engined bombers on their way to attack French targets.

Morale – the emotional well-being of people.

TURNING POINTS: The Battle of Britain

The Battle of Britain was Germany's attempt to win control of the skies over England and the Channel. Victory in the air was necessary before any invasion began. The Germans had 2,800 aircraft that set out to destroy Britain's 700 fighters. Britain's fate rested upon "the Few"—the pilots who flew Hurricane (at right) and Spitfire fighters. On October 31, after 114 days of combat, Germany gave in. The Germans had lost 1,733 aircraft. The RAF had lost 828 aircraft—but had saved Britain's air defenses.

JUNE 30 Channel Islands

German troops invade the Channel Islands. The islands are the only British home territory occupied during the war.

JULY 1 Atlantic Ocean

Using French ports as bases, U-boats inflict serious losses on Allied convoys carrying supplies across the Atlantic. This so-called "Happy Time" lasts until October.

JULY 3 Algeria

Fearing that they will be used by Germany, British warships attack French vessels at Oran and Mers-el-Kebir, Algeria. French naval forces in Alexandria, Egypt, are disarmed on the 7th. Meanwhile, two French battleships, nine destroyers, and other craft are captured in Britain.

JULY 10 Britain

The Battle of Britain begins. Hermann Goering, the Nazi Air Force chief, orders attacks on Allied shipping and ports in the English Channel. The air attacks soon reduce the movement of Allied ships in the English Channel.

Allied vessels under German air attack in the English Channel.

Convoy – a number of ships or vehicles traveling together.

JULY 16 Germany

Hitler reveals a plan to invade Britain, codenamed Operation Sealion. It requires control of Channel ports where the invasion force can board ships. British warplanes must also be destroyed so that the troops can cross the Channel safely.

JULY 21 Soviet Union

The Soviets annexe (take over) Lithuania, Latvia, and Estonia.

AUGUST 13–17 Britain

"Eagle Day" begins a four-day German air attack against British airfields and factories.

AUGUST 24–25 Britain

The Luftwaffe inflicts serious losses on the RAF during attacks on its main bases in southeast England. Fighter Command, which runs the British air war, is close to breaking point.

A German Heinkel bomber flies over London during the "Blitz."

AUGUST 26–29 Germany

The RAF launches night raids on Berlin and other cities. The Germans bomb London in revenge, but the raids mean that many German aircraft remain in Germany.

SEPTEMBER 7 Britain

Full-scale bombing raids on London—the "Blitz"—begin; they last 57 days.

SEPTEMBER 13–18 Egypt

An Italian force of 250,000 invades British-controlled Egypt and advance slowly.

SEPTEMBER 20–22 Atlantic Ocean

German U-boats launch their first "Wolf Pack" operation, sinking 12 Allied ships. A "pack" brings together some 15 to 20 U-boats for an attack on a convoy.

EYEWITNESS: John Beard, RAF pilot, Battle of Britain

"I saw my first burst (of gunfire) go in and, just as I was on top of him and turning away, I noticed a red glow inside the bomber. I turned tightly into position again and now saw several short tongues of flame lick out along the fuselage. Then he went down in a spin, blanketed with smoke and with pieces flying off."

"Wolf Pack" – a group of 15 to 20 German U-boats.

SEPTEMBER 27 Germany, Italy, and Japan
All three countries agree the Tripartite Pact. They will all fight any state that declares war on any one of them.

OCTOBER 28 Greece
Italy demands to be allowed to occupy Greece for as long as the war lasts. Italian troops invade Greece from Albania, meeting Greek resistance.

NOVEMBER 5 United States
President Franklin D. Roosevelt is elected for an unprecedented third term.

NOVEMBER 11–12 Mediterranean Sea
The Battle of Taranto. British torpedo aircraft destroy three Italian battleships and damage two vessels. British cruisers also sink four vessels in the Strait of Otranto.

NOVEMBER 14 Britain
The industrial city of Coventry is bombed by 449 German aircraft. The raid kills 500 civilians and leaves thousands homeless.

A German photograph of Coventry. This English city was bombed in 1940.

DECEMBER 9–11 Egypt
The British begin their first offensive in North Africa. The Western Desert Force—31,000 men supported by aircraft and naval gunfire—attacks Italian positions. Some 34,000 Italians are taken prisoner as they retreat rapidly from Egypt.

KEY PEOPLE: Benito Mussolini

Benito Mussolini (1883–1945) was the fascist dictator of Italy. After coming to power in 1922, he put down opposition and promised to create a new Roman empire. He followed his ally, Adolf Hitler, into World War II. Soon, however, Italy suffered a number of defeats. It had to depend on German military help. In July 1943, Mussolini was fired by the king. He was rescued by German troops, but shot by Italian communists in April 1945.

Ultimatum – a demand made by one country on another.

EYEWITNESS: Ernie Pyle, U.S. journalist, London 1940

"Shortly after the sirens wailed you could hear the Germans grinding overhead. In my room, with its black curtains drawn across the windows, you could feel the shake from the guns. You could hear the boom, crump, crump, crump, of heavy bombs at their work of tearing buildings apart. They were not too far away. Flames seemed to whip hundreds of feet into the air. St. Paul's was surrounded by fire, but it came through."

JANUARY 2, 1941, United States
President Franklin D. Roosevelt announces a program to produce 200 freighters, called "Liberty" ships, to support the Allied Atlantic convoys.

FEBRUARY 3 Atlantic Ocean
The German battlecruisers *Scharnhorst* and *Gneisenau* start sinking Allied merchant ships in the Atlantic. They sink 22 vessels before returning to base on March 22.

FEBRUARY 14 North Africa
German General Erwin Rommel's skilled Afrika Korps arrives at Tripoli in Libya to help the Italians.

MARCH 11 United States
President Franklin D. Roosevelt signs the Lend-Lease Act. The act allows Britain to obtain supplies without having to pay for them immediately in cash.

MARCH 28–29 Mediterranean Sea
The Battle of Cape Matapan. The Italian and British fleets clash in the Aegean Sea. Five Italian ships are sunk and 3,000 men killed. The British lose just one aircraft.

APRIL 6–15 Yugoslavia
German forces, with Italian and Hungarian support, invade Yugoslavia.

APRIL 17 Yugoslavia
Yugoslavia surrenders to Germany. But guerrilla forces, called partisans, continue to resist the occupiers.

The Italian battleship *Vittorio Veneto* in action at the Battle of Cape Matapan.

Partisan – a soldier who fights behind enemy lines.

21

TURNING POINTS: Lend-Lease

After the fall of France in June 1940, U.S. President Franklin D. Roosevelt wanted to supply Britain with weapons to keep fighting Germany. Britain could not afford to pay, however. In March 1941, the U.S. Congress passed the Lend-Lease Act. The act gave Roosevelt power to supply goods (including ships, at right) and services to countries friendly to the United States. The other countries did not have to pay right away. Almost $13 billion of goods had been allocated under the arrangement by November 1941.

APRIL 18–21 Greece

Greek positions are collapsing rapidly as the Germans advance. British troops sent to help the Greeks are also falling back to the southern coast to be evacuated to Crete.

MAY 3–19 Ethiopia

The Battle of Amba Alagi in northern Ethiopia ends in Italian surrender to the British. Some 230, 000 Italians have been killed or captured in East Africa.

MAY 10 Britain

Rudolf Hess, deputy leader of Germany, flies secretly to Scotland on an unofficial mission to ask Britain to allow Germany a "free hand" in Europe. In return, the Nazis will leave Britain and its empire alone. The British imprison him.

MAY 10–11 Britain

In the largest raid of the "Blitz," London is attacked by 507 bombers. Since September 1940, 39,678 people have died and 46,119 people have been injured by the raids.

MAY 20–22 Crete

Some 23,000 German paratroopers attack Crete. They come under attack from the 42,000 British, New Zealand, Australian, and Greek troops on the island. But the Germans gain enough of a footing to allow them to land reinforcements.

The German battleship *Bismarck* opens fire on the British ship HMS *Hood*.

Paratrooper – a soldier who jumps from an aircraft with a parachute.

EYEWITNESS: Esmond Knight, HMS *Prince of Wales*, May 24, 1941

"I just did not believe what I saw—*Hood* had literally been blown to pieces, and just before she was totally enveloped in that ghastly pall of smoke I noticed that she was firing her last salvo. I felt quite sick inside and turned away and looked towards George, where he was standing with his hands limply to his sides, staring like a man in a dream."

MAY 23–27 Atlantic Ocean
British warships find the German battleship *Bismarck* in the Denmark Straits between Iceland and Greenland. The *Bismarck* sinks the battlecruiser *Hood* and damages the battleship *Prince of Wales*—but is then sunk by gunfire and torpedoes.

MAY 28–31 Crete
The Germans capture Crete. British losses are 3,753 men, while Germany has 3,985 men killed or missing.

JUNE 15–17 North Africa
The British launch Operation Battleaxe to relieve the Libyan port of Tobruk, where British troops are surrounded by the Afrika Korps. The operation halts after the British lose 90 of their 190 tanks.

JUNE 22 Soviet Union
Germany launches Operation Barbarossa, the invasion of the Soviet Union, with three million men. Army Group North strikes toward the Baltic and Leningrad. Army Group Center aims to take Smolensk and then Moscow. Army Group South advances toward the Ukraine and the Caucasus.

German air attacks quickly destroy 1,800 Soviet aircraft on the ground.

JULY 4 Yugoslavia
Joseph Broz, known as "Tito," emerges as the leader of the Yugoslav partisans.

JULY 16 Soviet Union
Around 300,000 Red Army troops and 3,200 tanks are trapped near Smolensk.

JULY 31 Germany
Reinhard Heydrich, head of the SS secret police, is ordered to plan the destruction of Europe's Jews. This "Final Solution" will lead to the killing of millions of people.

Soviet soldiers surrender to German troops during Operation Barbarossa.

Surrender – to stop fighting and give in to the enemy.

Female recruits to the Soviet forces march through Moscow.

British tanks suffer heavy losses to German antitank guns, but Rommel retreats. This relieves the pressure on Tobruk.

NOVEMBER 26 Pacific Ocean
A Japanese fleet of six aircraft carriers and other warships begins a mission to destroy the U.S. Pacific Fleet at Pearl Harbor, Hawaii. The ships remain undetected by maintaining radio silence. Japan's war aims are to destroy U.S. warships in the region and then to seize lands in the Pacific and East Asia. They intend to create a "Greater East Asian Co-Prosperity Sphere" to supply Japan with resources.

SEPTEMBER 3 Poland
Successful experiments to kill Jewish prisoners using gas chambers are carried out in Auschwitz concentration camp. They will lead to the widespread use of Zyclon-B gas to kill Jews.

SEPTEMBER 4 Atlantic Ocean
A U-boat mistakes the U.S. destroyer *Greer* for a British vessel and attacks it. U.S. warships are ordered to "shoot on sight" any U-boats they see.

SEPTEMBER 19 Soviet Union
The Germans capture Kiev, killing or capturing 665,000 Soviet soldiers.

SEPTEMBER 30 Soviet Union
The Germans begin Operation Typhoon, the attack on Moscow.

NOVEMBER 18–26 North Africa
The British Eighth Army in Egypt launches Operation Crusader to relieve Tobruk.

EYEWITNESS: Major Lozak, Leningrad, December 1941

"I have lived in Leningrad all my life. I'd walk for a while, and then sit down for a rest. Many a time I saw a man suddenly collapse on the snow. There was nothing I could do. One just walked on. And, on the way back, I would see a vague human form covered with snow on the spot where, in the morning, I had seen a man fall down."

U-boat – a German submarine.

TURNING POINTS: Rationing

The war brought international trade to a near halt. Countries such as Britain could not import enough food. In the Soviet Union, where farmland was damaged by fighting, thousands of people starved to death. All the countries involved in the war introduced rationing, which limited how much food people could buy. People had ration books that allowed them to get a set amount of food each day or week. As the war went on, food and water (at right) became more difficult to get. Rations were cut.

DECEMBER 7 Hawaii

Some 183 Japanese aircraft attack the U.S. Pacific Fleet at Pearl Harbor, Hawaii. They destroy six battleships and 188 aircraft, damage or sink 10 other vessels, and kill 2,000 people. The Japanese lose 29 aircraft.

U.S. warships on fire at Pearl Harbor following the Japanese attack.

DECEMBER 8 Soviet Union

Adolf Hitler halts the advance on Moscow for the winter. The German panzers cannot operate in the freezing temperatures.

DECEMBER 10 Pacific Ocean

About 90 Japanese aircraft sink the British warships *Prince of Wales* and *Repulse*: 730 sailors drown.

DECEMBER 11 Germany and Italy

Germany and Italy declare war on the United States. The United States then declares war on Germany and Italy.

DECEMBER 18–19 Egypt

An Italian attack upon the British Mediterranean Fleet in Alexandria, Egypt, sinks the battleships *Queen Elizabeth* and *Valiant*. The Italians use "human torpedoes," midget submarines each driven by two operators.

Panzer – German word for a tank.

JANUARY 5, 1942, Soviet Union

Joseph Stalin orders a massive counterattack against the German invaders. The Red Army has initial success and captures trains, food, and munitions. But then German forces set up well-defended areas known as "hedgehogs," which halt the Soviet attacks.

JANUARY 10–11 Dutch East Indies

Japanese troops attack the Dutch East Indies to capture the oilfields of the island chain.

JANUARY 13 Atlantic Ocean

Germany's U-boats launch Operation Drum Roll, a series of attacks on shipping off the east coast of the United States. Some 20 ships are sunk in the first month.

JANUARY 16–19 Germany

Hitler sacks more than 30 of his senior generals; he is impatient that they want to withdraw in the face of Soviet attacks on the Eastern Front.

Victorious Japanese troops celebrate their conquest of Singapore.

JANUARY 20 Germany

The Wannsee Conference in Berlin. SS deputy leader Reinhard Heydrich reveals his plans for what is termed the "Final Solution" to the so-called "Jewish problem." The extermination of Jews in Europe becomes central to Nazi war plans.

KEY WEAPONS: Atlantic convoys

Convoys helped protect Allied merchant ships against enemy attack. A large group—often more than 50 vessels—was accompanied by warships. The main threat to convoys came from U-boats, but antisubmarine measures gradually improved. Cooperation between naval and air forces also improved. It was helped by new tactics, and scientific innovations, such as radar. In the North Atlantic alone, the Germans sank 2,232 Allied vessels. But they lost 785 U-boats in return.

Extermination – the murder of an entire people.

The German heavy cruiser *Prinz Eugen* during the "Channel Dash."

FEBRUARY 8 Singapore
Japanese troops land on the British-held island of Singapore. The British surrender on February 14 when the water supply is cut. The defenders have lost 138,000 men.

FEBRUARY 11–12 North Sea
In the so-called Channel Dash, the German battlecruisers *Gneisenau* and *Scharnhorst* and the heavy cruiser *Prinz Eugen* leave Brest. They speed through the English Channel into the North Sea before British warships and aircraft can stop them.

FEBRUARY 27–29 Java Sea
The Battle of the Java Sea. Five Allied cruisers and nine destroyers fight 17 Japanese warships. Five Allied cruisers and five destroyers are sunk. The Japanese lose only one cruiser in this victory.

MARCH 28–29 France
British commandos attack the St. Nazaire dry-dock, used by the Germans to repair warships. The British fill an old destroyer and ram the lock gates, blowing them up. But 144 men die in the raid and many more are captured.

APRIL 9 Philippines
Major General Jonathan Wainright, commanding the U.S. and Filipino forces, surrenders to the Japanese. Some 78,000 U.S. and Filipino troops are forced to make a 65-mile (104-km) march without food or water. Many die along the way.

APRIL 18 Japan
Lieutenant Colonel James Doolittle leads 16 U.S. B-25 bombers, launched from the aircraft carrier *Hornet*, on a daring mission to strike targets in Japan, including the capital Tokyo. The raid alarms Japan's leaders, who decide to seek a battle to destroy U.S. naval power in the Pacific.

EYEWITNESS: Robert Carse, British merchant seaman, 1942

"They came early: the Heinkels, the Messerschmitts, the Stukas, the Junkers 89s, and all told there were 105 of them over us during that day's fight that was to last twenty hours. All around us, as so slowly we kept on going, the pure blue of the sea was mottled blackish with the greasy patches of their bomb discharges. Our ship was missed closely time and again. We drew our breaths in a kind of gasping-choke."

Commandos – special forces soldiers.

A German panzer commander at the Battle of Gazala in North Africa.

Rommel has 630 tanks, but they suffer serious fuel problems until the Italians break through the British Gazala Line to bring up fuel supplies on the 31st.

MAY 31 Germany

Britain launches its first "1,000 bomber raid" on Cologne, where 59,000 people are left homeless. The British lose 40 aircraft.

JUNE 4 Pacific Ocean

The Battle of Midway. Japan's fleet of 165 warships, including eight carriers, aims to seize the U.S. base at Midway Island and destroy the U.S. Pacific Fleet. The U.S. Navy has fewer ships, but has managed to gather three carriers. In the battle, the Japanese lose four carriers and 275 aircraft.

JUNE 10–13 North Africa

The Battle of Gazala. German attacks force the British Eighth Army to withdraw east. Rommel's way is open to Tobruk.

MAY 8 Pacific Ocean

In the Battle of the Coral Sea, the U.S. Navy loses a carrier. The Japanese lose a smaller carrier, but large numbers of aircraft.

MAY 26–31 North Africa

The Battle of Gazala. Rommel attacks the British Eighth Army, which has 850 tanks.

KEY PEOPLE: Joseph Stalin

Joseph Stalin (1879–1953) was communist dictator of the Soviet Union. He was stunned when his former ally Hitler invaded in June 1941, but called on Russians to defend "Mother Russia." Stalin demanded that Britain and the United States open a "second front" in western Europe to relieve the Soviet Union. The Allies also sent him supplies. After the war, Stalin created communist "buffer states" around the Soviet Union.

"Buffer state" – a country between two enemy states.

EYEWITNESS: Mitsuo Fuchida on the *Akagi*, Battle of Midway, 1942

"The raiders closed in from both sides, barely skimming over the water. Flying in single columns, they were within five miles and seemed to be aiming straight for *Akagi*. I watched in breathless suspense, thinking how impossible it would be to dodge all their torpedoes. But these raiders, too, without protective escorts, were already being engaged by our fighters. There was wild cheering and whistling as the raiders went."

JUNE 21 North Africa
Rommel captures Tobruk. Some 30,000 men are seized, together with rations and fuel.

JUNE 28 Soviet Union
Germany launches Operation Blue, a summer offensive into southern Russia. Its target is the Russian oilfields in the Caucasus region.

JULY 4−10 Soviet Union
After a two-month siege, the Germans capture the port of Sevastopol. About 90,000 Red Army troops are taken prisoner.

AUGUST 7−21 Guadalcanal
The U.S. 1st Marine Division lands on Guadalcanal. Fierce fighting breaks out against Japanese defenders to control the airstrip at Henderson Field.

AUGUST 9 Pacific Ocean
The Battle of Savo Island. The Japanese sink four U.S. cruisers. This is a heavy defeat for the U.S. Navy in the Pacific.

AUGUST 19 France
A force of 5,000 Canadian, 1,000 British, and 50 U.S. troops attack the port of Dieppe. It is a disaster: 4,000 men are killed or captured.

AUGUST 23 Soviet Union
A raid by 600 German bombers on Stalingrad claims thousands of lives.

SEPTEMBER 2 Poland
The Nazis are "clearing" the Jewish Warsaw Ghetto. Over 50,000 Jews have been killed.

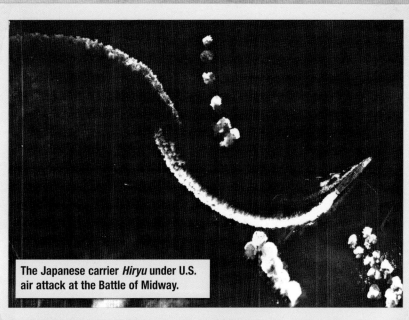

The Japanese carrier *Hiryu* under U.S. air attack at the Battle of Midway.

Ghetto – part of a city where Jews were forced to live.

TURNING POINTS: Strategic Bombing

Strategic bombing is the name given to air attacks against an enemy's industry and population. However, while the Allied strategic bombing of Germany's oil industry and transportation system played a key role near the end of the war, the bombers (at right) were never capable of defeating the enemy alone. Raids against Japan began in 1944. They reduced a number of cities to ashes—but Japan did not surrender until the nuclear strikes in 1945.

OCTOBER 23 North Africa

The Battle of El Alamein begins when 195,000 Allied troops attack 104,000 Axis soldiers. Axis resistance is fierce.

NOVEMBER 2–24 North Africa

The Battle of El Alamein. Rommel is forced to retreat. Germany and Italy have lost 59,000 men killed, wounded, or captured. The Allies have suffered 13,000 losses. El Alamein is the first major defeat suffered by German forces during the war.

NOVEMBER 19 Soviet Union

General Georgi Zhukov launches a Soviet attack to relieve the city of Stalingrad, which is occupied by the Germans. The rapid pincer movement traps the Germans fighting in the city. The German front collapses.

DECEMBER 19 Soviet Union

German attempts fail to rescue the Sixth Army trapped in Stalingrad. Within the city, German troops are suffering severe hardships due to the bitterly cold winter weather and food shortages.

Soldiers of the British Eighth Army attacking at the Battle of El Alamein.

Strategic – something that is useful in achieving a long-term goal.

EYEWITNESS: General Theodore Roosevelt, North Africa, March 1943

"Among our troubles were the dive-bombers. They came down on us constantly. Once I was caught in a valley by a raid. A bomb hit within twelve paces of where I was lying. My helmet was struck by a fragment and knocked galley-west, but I was unhurt though a couple of men were killed. The following day the enemy counterattack came. I could see it all."

JANUARY 10–31, 1943, Guadalcanal
Some 50,000 U.S. troops attack the Japanese defenders. The Japanese are starving, and many are sick. The high command has therefore decided to leave Guadalcanal.

JANUARY 13 Papua New Guinea
The Japanese lose control of the Kokoda Trail, a major route across the Owen Stanley mountains. This cuts off their access to Port Moresby, which they were planning to use as an air base.

JANUARY 18 Poland
Jewish fighters in the Warsaw Ghetto begin attacking German troops.

FEBRUARY 2 Soviet Union
The siege of Stalingrad ends when 93,000 German troops surrender. The Sixth Army has been unable to cope with the strain of food shortages and constant attacks.

FEBRUARY 14–22 North Africa
The Battle of Kasserine Pass. Rommel's attack causes widespread panic among inexperienced U.S. troops. Rommel loses 2,000 men; the Americans 10,000.

FEBRUARY 16 Germany
Students demonstrate against Hitler's regime in Munich. The protestors are led by brother and sister Hans and Sophie Scholl, leaders of the anti-Nazi White Rose student group at the University of Munich. They fail in their plan to start a revolt that will topple the government. The Scholls are arrested and executed on the 21st.

FEBRUARY 18 Burma
Brigadier Orde Wingate launches the first British Chindit mission. A 3,000-strong force parachutes behind Japanese lines to begin raids on supply lines. However, the six-week mission is only partly successful.

British Chindits ready to be flown behind enemy lines in Burma.

Chindit – a British soldier who fought behind Japanese lines in Burma.

MARCH 2–5 Bismarck Sea

In the Battle of the Bismarck Sea, Allied warships sink eight Japanese transports and four destroyers. The Allies lose six aircraft and the Japanese 25.

MARCH 14 Soviet Union

German forces under General Erich von Manstein destroy the Soviet Third Tank Army. The Soviets have now abandoned nearly 6,000 square miles (9,600 sq km) of newly-won ground in the face of Manstein's armored attack. This has prevented a total Axis collapse on the Eastern Front.

MARCH 15 Soviet Union

The Germans recapture Kharkov and Belgorod three days later. The victory encourages the Germans to launch Operation Citadel, a plan to destroy 500,000 Red Army troops around the city of Kursk.

APRIL 12 Soviet Union

The Germans find a mass grave in Katyn Forest. It contains the bodies of 10,000

A Japanese merchant ship is attacked by U.S. aircraft in the Pacific.

Polish army officers executed by the Soviet secret police in 1939.

APRIL 17 Germany

The U.S. Eighth Army Air Force attacks Bremen. Sixteen of the 115 B-17 Flying Fortress bombers are shot down.

MAY 13 North Africa

Axis forces surrender to the Allies. Some 620,000 Axis casualties and prisoners have been lost in North Africa.

KEY PEOPLE: Franklin D. Roosevelt

Franklin D. Roosevelt (1882–1945) was U.S. president from 1933 to 1945. He turned the United States into an "arsenal of democracy" to supply the Allies with weapons. When the United States entered the war in 1941, Roosevelt made the key decision to follow a "Germany First" strategy. U.S. troops would concentrate on defeating Hitler rather than defeating Japan. Roosevelt died three weeks before the end of the war in Europe.

Strategy – a long-term plan of action.

EYEWITNESS: General Mellenthin, Kursk, 1943

"The entire area had been laid with mines; and the Russian defense along the whole line was supported by tanks operating with the advantages of high ground. Our assault troops suffered considerable casualties, and 3 Panzer Division had to beat off counterattacks. In spite of several massive bombing attacks by the Luftwaffe, the Russian defensive fire did not decrease to any extent."

MAY 16–17 Germany
Dams on the Möhne and Eder rivers are smashed by British Lancaster bombers using specially-designed "bouncing bombs." The raid badly disrupts power and water supplies to the Ruhr, one of Germany's most important industrial regions. The British lose eight aircraft in the attack, but it is a great morale boost.

MAY 16 Poland
The Warsaw Ghetto uprising ends. It has been brutally crushed by the Germans, who have used flamethrowers to burn out Jewish fighters. A total of around 14,000 Jews have been killed. Another 22,000 are sent to concentration camps, and 20,000 to labor camps.

JUNE 10 Germany
Operation Pointblank is launched. This series of attacks on Germany by British and U.S. bomber forces will last until the Allies invade France in June 1944. U.S. strategy concentrates on daylight precision raids to destroy Germany's air forces and its aircraft industry. British attacks focus on night-time saturation bombing to undermine Germany's economy and civilian morale.

JULY 5 Soviet Union
The Battle of Kursk. More than 6,000 German and Soviet tanks and assault guns take part in the war's largest armored battle. The Germans make little progress against Soviet antitank defenses.

JULY 9 Sicily
U.S. and British troops invade the island.

JULY 12–13 Soviet Union
At Kursk, the Soviets launch a counterattack around the village of Prokhorovka. In the tank battle that follows, the Germans are defeated. During the whole battle, they have lost more than 550 tanks and 500,000 men killed, wounded, or missing.

German armored personnel carriers and assault guns at Kursk.

Counterattack – an attack by a defending force.

The results of the British bombing raid on the city of Hamburg.

JULY 24–AUGUST 2 Germany

A series of massive British bombing raids on Hamburg leave about 50,000 people dead and 800,000 homeless.

JULY 25 Italy

The king of Italy fires Benito Mussolini, who is arrested. Marshal Pietro Badoglio forms a new government. Badoglio hopes that the Allies will quickly occupy most of Italy before it falls under German control.

AUGUST 17 Sicily

The capture of Messina marks the Allied victory on Sicily. About 10,000 Germans have been killed or captured. The Italians have lost 132,000 men, mainly as prisoners. Sicily is now a springboard for an invasion of Italy.

AUGUST 22–23 Soviet Union

Kharkov is retaken by the Red Army. The Soviets now threaten the Ukraine.

SEPTEMBER 9 Italy

Lieutenant General Mark Clark's U.S. Fifth Army lands in southern Italy with the British X Corps.

SEPTEMBER 12 Italy

German airborne troops led by Lieutenant Colonel Otto Skorzeny rescue Mussolini from imprisonment in Gran Sasso.

SEPTEMBER 25 Soviet Union

The Soviets recapture Smolensk. Germany's Army Group Center is now falling back.

OCTOBER 12–22 Italy

U.S. forces make slow progress north in the face of bad weather. The British Eighth

EYEWITNESS: Robert Sherrod, Tarawa Atoll, November 1943

"We jumped into the little tractor boat and quickly settled on the deck. 'Oh, God, I'm scared,' said the little Marine, a telephone operator, who sat next to me forward in the boat. I gritted my teeth and tried to force a smile that would not come and tried to stop quivering all over (now I was shaking from fear). I said, in an effort to be reassuring, 'I'm scared, too.' I never made a more truthful statement in my life."

Corps – a military unit made up of several divisions.

TURNING POINTS: Resistance

In countries overrun by the Germans and Japanese, some people were determined to oppose the occupiers. Resistance involved demonstrations, strikes, gathering intelligence, helping escaped Allied prisoners of war, and sabotage. The dangers of fighting back against occupiers were great. Many captured Resistance fighters were tortured and killed. Resistance groups in Europe and East Asia helped the Allied victory— but in most cases they only came out into the open after the war (at right).

Army also advances north. The Germans have created strong defenses in central Italy, known as the Gustav Line.

OCTOBER 25 Burma
The Burma to Siam rail link is completed. It has been built by the Japanese using Allied prisoners and local people as labor. About 12,000 prisoners have died as a result of accidents, abuse, disease, and starvation.

NOVEMBER 6 Soviet Union
The Soviets take Kiev. The victory traps the German Seventeenth Army in the Crimea.

NOVEMBER 20 Gilbert Islands
Some 18,600 U.S. Marines land on Tarawa and Betio. More than 1,000 Marines are killed in fierce fighting before the islands are captured on the 23rd.

NOVEMBER 28 Iran
In Tehran, British Prime Minister Winston Churchill meets U.S. President Franklin D. Roosevelt and Soviet leader Joseph Stalin. They give priority to a cross-Channel invasion of German-occupied Europe and a landing in southern France in May 1944.

DECEMBER 26 Arctic Ocean
The Battle of the North Cape. British warships sink the German battleship *Scharnhorst*. Some 1,800 Germans drown.

Soviet Red Army troops and artillery in action on the outskirts of Kiev.

Sabotage – destruction of an enemy's property.

1944

JANUARY 14–17, 1944, Soviet Union
Red Army attacks on the German forces besieging Leningrad result in heavy fighting and a German retreat. Some 830,000 civilians have died during the three-year-long siege.

JANUARY 22 Italy
The Allies attempt to overcome the Gustav Line by landing troops behind it at Anzio, on Italy's western coast. Commanded by U.S. General John Lucas, the initial attack meets virtually no resistance. The road to Rome is open—but Lucas orders his forces to dig in and create defensive positions.

JANUARY 30 Marshall Islands
The Americans begin a planned conquest of the Marshall Islands that aims to attack Japanese-held islands and Japanese air bases. Operation Flintlock begins with an amphibious assault on an undefended island in Majuro Atoll.

American dive-bombers return from attacking Japanese ships.

FEBRUARY 1–4 Marshall Islands
American forces launch an amphibious assault against Kwajalein Atoll. Some 40,000 U.S. Marines and infantry land on the islands of Roi, Namur, and Kwajalein. Total Japanese losses are 11,612 men killed. The Americans lose more than 1,000.

FEBRUARY 4–24 Burma
The Japanese launch Operation Ha-Go to force the Allies back to the Indian border.

TURNING POINTS: Women at war
Women on the home front did not only have to complete their usual daily chores. With men away fighting, many also had to go to work to support the war effort. Women in Germany became workers and, later in the war, fighters (at right). In the Soviet Union, women fought in the army or flew warplanes. In America and Britain, women worked in factories producing weapons and aircraft. For many women, this was their first employment. After the war, many chose not to go back to being housewives.

Amphibious assault – an attack by soldiers who land from the sea.

EYEWITNESS: Leon Degrelle, SS comander, Russia, 1944

"Snow fell endlessly in the evening. It was soon a foot high. Twenty or thirty thousand people waited in our village for some kind of military end to the drama, with no accommodation. Oblivious to the danger, the people stood out in the open in groups around fires they had lit in the snow. Lying out in this biting cold would have meant certain death."

Initial Japanese attacks are successful, but Allied troops then fight back.

FEBRUARY 18–22 Marshall Islands
U.S. forces complete their conquest of the islands with the seizure of Eniwetok Atoll. The Japanese lose 3,400 killed.

MARCH 7–8 India/Burma
Operation U-Go begins; the Japanese assault aims to drive the Allies back into India by attacking their bases at Imphal and Kohima.

MARCH 20–22 Italy
Allied attacks fail to overcome Monte Cassino, part of the Gustav Line.

MAY 9 Soviet Union
The Red Army liberates the Black Sea port of Sevastopol. It is a crushing defeat for the German defenders, who have lost 100,000 men killed and captured.

MAY 11–18 Italy
The Allies break through the Gustav Line near Monte Cassino. On the 17th, the Germans evacuate the monastery at Monte Cassino to avoid becoming surrounded. Next day, the Polish 12th Podolski Regiment storms the ruined buildings.

JUNE 3 India
The 64-day Battle of Kohima ends with a Japanese withdrawal. The fighting has been some of the most savage of the whole war. In the end, however, it is a lack of supplies that forces the Japanese to fall back, rather than British and Indian attacks.

JUNE 3–5 Italy
The Germans abandon Rome. U.S. troops enter the city on the 5th. It is the first Axis capital to be captured.

The shell-blasted remains of the monastery of Monte Cassino.

Marine – a soldier based on a ship who fights on land.

TURNING POINTS: Kamikaze

Kamikaze is Japanese for "Divine Wind." It was a suicide tactic used by the Japanese to destroy U.S. shipping by crashing explosive-filled aircraft into vessels. The tactic was first used in the Battle of Leyte Gulf in October 1944. Kamikaze pilots tried to hit the deck of their target to cause maximum damage (against carriers, they aimed for the central elevator, seen at right). During the Okinawa battles in 1945, Japanese pilots flew 1,900 suicide missions.

JUNE 6 France
D-Day. The Allied invasion of Normandy, codenamed Operation Overlord, begins. Paratroopers land to seize key inland targets and seaborne forces storm five beaches. By the end of the day, the Allies have a toehold in Europe at a cost of 2,500 dead.

JUNE 10 France
German soldiers kill 642 civilians in the town of Oradour-sur-Glane. The atrocity is a retaliation for attacks on a German SS Panzer division by the French Resistance.

JUNE 13 France
A Tiger tank commanded by Lieutenant Michael Wittmann destroys 27 British tanks and armored vehicles in a battle at the village of Villers-Bocage, Normandy.

JUNE 19–21 Philippine Sea
The Battle of the Philippine Sea. The Japanese Combined Fleet is defeated by the U.S. 5th Fleet. It loses three aircraft carriers and 460 combat aircraft and pilots in what U.S. pilots name the "Great Marianas Turkey Shoot."

JUNE 22 Soviet Union
The Red Army launches Operation Bagration against German Army Group Center. The Soviets enjoy a four-to-one superiority in tanks and aircraft.

U.S. soldiers wade ashore under fire on D-Day, the invasion of Normandy.

Retaliation – revenge for a previous event.

JUNE 30 Britain

To date, 2,000 German V1 "Flying Bombs" have been launched against England, mostly against London.

JULY 9 Saipan

U.S. troops secure the island. At least 8,000 Japanese troops and civilians have committed suicide rather than surrender to the Americans.

JULY 20 Germany

German officers try to kill Adolf Hitler. Count Schenk von Stauffenberg plants a bomb in a conference room, but fails to kill Hitler. The failure of the plot results in the arrest, torture, and execution of dozens of suspects.

AUGUST 1 Poland

The Warsaw uprising—38,000 soldiers of the Polish Home Army fight the Germans.

AUGUST 10 Marianas Islands

Japanese resistance on Guam finally ends after fierce fighting. However, the last

Hitler (center) shows Mussolini (left) the bomb-damaged conference room.

Japanese soldier on the island does not give himself up until 1960.

AUGUST 25 France

General Dietrich von Choltitz, commander of the German garrison of Paris, surrenders the city to the Allies.

SEPTEMBER 2 Finland

Finland, exhausted by the war, accepts a peace treaty with the Soviet Union. The Finns cut relations with Germany.

EYEWITNESS: Jim Irving, U.S. Army, Omaha Beach, June 6, 1944

"Our main objective was to clear eight lanes for landing craft on the two beaches. This was impossible as the infantry and tank battalion landing in front of us were pinned down at the water's edge. At 0900 the beach master stopped additional vehicles due to congestion on the beach. Only engineers and infantry were allowed to be incoming on Omaha Beach until, at 11 am, with all troops on shore we cleared the beach."

Uprising – a revolt against a ruler.

General MacArthur (second from left) wades ashore in the Philippines.

OCTOBER 2 Poland

After a two-month battle, the last Poles in Warsaw surrender to the Germans. Polish deaths number 150,000.

OCTOBER 20 Philippines

As the U.S. Sixth Army lands on Leyte Island, General Douglas MacArthur wades ashore. He keeps a promise he made two years earlier: "I shall return."

OCTOBER 23–26 Philippines

The Japanese Combined Fleet is defeated at the Battle of Leyte Gulf. It loses 500 aircraft, 28 ships, and a submarine. U.S. losses are 200 aircraft and six ships.

DECEMBER 16 Belgium

Hitler begins Operation Watch on the Rhine, which aims to capture Antwerp in Belgium. The Germans attack in thick fog. At first they advance, but U.S. paratroopers hold out in Bastogne.

SEPTEMBER 17 Holland

Operation Market Garden, an Allied attack on occupied Holland, begins. Paratroopers land near Arnhem, Eindhoven, and Nijmegen to seize key bridges. But the Germans are waiting.The Allies suffer heavy casualties.

SEPTEMBER 22–25 Holland

The paratroopers retreat from Arnhem. The British alone have lost 2,500 dead.

TURNING POINTS: The Holocaust

The Holocaust was the Nazi program to exterminate Europe's Jews and other "undesirables." The Nazis saw the Jews as the enemy of "Aryan" Germans. They sent Jews from occupied countries to concentration camps, where they were used as slave labor. In extermination camps, hundreds of thousands of people died in gas chambers. The six million victims included not just Jews but Roma (gypsies), homosexuals, and the Nazis' political opponents.

Destroyer – a small, fast warship.

EYEWITNESS: James Fahey, U.S. Navy, October 1944

"It was quite a sight. Japanese planes were coming at us from all directions. Before the attack started we did not know that they were suicide planes, with no intention of returning to their base. They had one thing in mind and that was to crash into our ships, bombs and all. You have to blow them up; to damage them doesn't mean much."

JANUARY 9, 1945, Philippines
Units of the U.S. Sixth Army make unopposed landings on the island of Luzon.

JANUARY 12–17 Poland
The Red Army begins its Vistula–Oder Offensive against the Germans. Soviet forces totalling more than two million men make rapid advances along the whole front.

JANUARY 27 Poland
The Red Army liberates the Nazi death camp at Auschwitz. The SS has evacuated the camp nine days previously, leaving behind a few hundred sick inmates in the camp's hospital block.

JANUARY 28 Belgium
The Ardennes Offensive has cost the Germans 100,000 killed, wounded, and captured. The Americans have lost 81,000 killed, wounded, or captured. The Germans have also lost 800 tanks.

JANUARY 30 Germany
Soviet forces reach the Oder River, only 100 miles (160 km) from Berlin. The Red Army has advanced 355 miles (568 km) and liberated all of Poland and a large part of Czechoslovakia. Its offensive has inflicted losses of 500,000 dead, wounded, or captured on the Germans.

FEBRUARY 3 Philippines
U.S. forces begin an attack on the capital, Manila, which is defended by 17,000 Japanese troops. The Japanese garrison destroy the city in the "Rape of Manila;" after a month's fighting, it is wiped out.

FEBRUARY 4 Soviet Union
Joseph Stalin, President Franklin D. Roosevelt, and Prime Minister Winston Churchill meet at Yalta in the Crimea to discuss postwar Europe. The "Big Three" decide that Germany will be divided into four zones, administered by Britain, France, the United States, and the Soviet Union.

Churchill (left), Roosevelt (center), and Stalin (right) at the Yalta Conference.

Liberate – to set free.

KEY WEAPONS: The Atomic Bomb

The atomic bomb used the energy released by splitting atoms to start a chain reaction that produced a huge explosion. The secret American program to make the bomb, codenamed the Manhattan Project, began in December 1941 at Los Alamos in New Mexico. It involved over 60,000 workers, led by J. Robert Oppenheimer. The new weapon had the destructive power of a raid by 2,000 B-29 bombers. The first bomb was successfully tested in New Mexico on July 16, 1945.

FEBRUARY 13–14 Germany
Some 805 British bombers attack Dresden. At least 50,000 people are killed. The next morning, the city is bombed again by 400 aircraft of the U.S. Eighth Army Air Force.

FEBRUARY 14 Germany
As a result of the Red Army's advance, half of the 2.3 million population of German East Prussia flee west. Thousands of civilians die from cold or exhaustion.

U.S. Marines in amphibious landing craft head for Iwo Jima's beaches.

FEBRUARY 17 Iwo Jima
Under the command of Lieutenant General Holland M. Smith, U.S. Marines land on the island of Iwo Jima. The attackers are pinned down by heavy artillery and small-arms fire from the 21,000-man Japanese garrison.

FEBRUARY 23 Iwo Jima
U.S. Marines raise the Stars and Stripes flag on the summit of Mount Suribachi. Fighting continues on the island, however.

MARCH 7 Japan
A U.S. bombing raid on Tokyo sets alight over 16 square miles (25.6 sq km) of the city and kills 100,000 people.

MARCH 16 Iwo Jima
The Americans declare the island secure. They have lost 6,821 soldiers and sailors dead. Of the 21,000 Japanese defenders, nearly 20,000 are dead.

Garrison – a military post.

EYEWITNESS: Dorothea von Schwanenfluegel, Berlin, April 1945

"The Soviets battled the German soldiers and drafted civilians street by street until we could hear explosions and rifle fire right in our immediate vicinity. Shots shattered our windows and shells exploded in our garden, and suddenly the Soviets were on our street. Shaken by the battle around us and numb with fear, we watched from behind the small cellar windows facing the street as the tanks and an endless convoy of troops rolled by."

MARCH 23 Germany
Field Marshal Bernard Montgomery's British forces begin crossing the Rhine River on the German border. Next day, U.S. troops begin crossing the river. German units offer little resistance.

APRIL 1 Okinawa
Operation Iceberg. The U.S. Tenth Army, with 183,000 men, lands on the island, which is only 325 miles (520 km) from Japan. The island's airfields and harbors will be used for the proposed Allied invasion of the Japanese mainland. Japanese defenders on the island number 80,000.

APRIL 7 Pacific Ocean
The *Yamato*, the world's largest battleship, is sunk by U.S. warplanes on its way to fight at Okinawa.

APRIL 9 Italy
The final campaign in Italy begins as the U.S. Fifth and British Eighth Armies attack German Army Group Center.

APRIL 12 United States
President Franklin D. Roosevelt dies of a brain hemorrhage in Warm Springs, Georgia. Vice President Harry S. Truman takes over as president.

APRIL 16 Germany
The Soviets attack Berlin. The Red Army has 2.5 million men, 41,600 guns, 6,250 tanks, and 7,500 combat aircraft. The German defenders have one million men, 10,400 guns, 1,500 tanks, and 3,300 aircraft.

U.S. troops and vehicles land on the island of Okinawa in early April 1945.

Hemorrhage – the bursting of a blood vessel.

43

TURNING POINTS: Casualties of War

No war in history cost as many lives as World War II. The Soviet Union lost more citizens than the other nations put together: 7.5 million military dead plus 15 million civilian deaths. Germany lost 2.8 million military dead and 500,000 civilians. Japan's total was 1.5 million military dead, plus 300,000 civilians who died in U.S. bombing raids. Other nations lost far fewer lives: the United States 292,000; Great Britain 397,762; France 210,600; and Italy 117,000. In all, civilian war deaths numbered 34 million.

APRIL 25 Germany

Berlin is surrounded by the Red Army. By the 27th, "Fortress Berlin" has been reduced to an east-to-west belt 10 miles (16 km) long by three miles (5 km) wide. Soviet rockets and bombs kill many defenders.

APRIL 28 Italy

Mussolini, trying to flee to Austria with his girlfriend Claretta Petacci, is captured by communist partisans. They are both shot.

APRIL 29 Italy

After a secret deal with the Americans, General Heinrich von Vietinghoff, German commander-in-chief in Italy, surrenders his forces to the Allies.

APRIL 30 Germany

Adolf Hitler and his wife Eva Braun commit suicide in Berlin. Hitler shoots himself, while Braun takes poison. Their bodies are later burned by the SS.

MAY 2 Germany

Following a savage three-day battle, the Reichstag in Berlin falls to the Red Army. Taking the city has cost the Soviets 300,000 men killed, wounded, or missing. The Germans have lost one million men.

MAY 3 Burma

Following 38 months of Japanese occupation, Rangoon falls to the Allies

Red Army troops fly the Soviet flag over the ruins of Berlin.

Reichstag – the German parliament.

The Japanese city of Hiroshima after it was devastated by an atomic bomb.

AUGUST 9 Manchuria

A Soviet offensive by 1.5 million men begins against the Japanese Kwantung Army.

AUGUST 9 Japan

An atomic bomb is dropped on Nagasaki. The bomb kills 35,000 people and injures 60,000. The Japanese decide to surrender.

AUGUST 23 Manchuria

The campaign in Manchuria ends in total Soviet victory. The Japanese have lost over 80,000 dead. Soviet losses are 8,000 men killed and 22,000 wounded.

without a fight. The city has been badly damaged by bombing. Some 100,000 civilians have been killed in total.

JUNE 22 Okinawa

Japanese resistance on the island ends. The battle has cost the Japanese 110,000 dead. U.S. Navy losses amount to 9,731, of whom 4,907 are killed, while the Tenth Army has suffered 7,613 men killed or missing and 31,807 wounded.

SEPTEMBER 2 Japan

Aboard the battleship *Missouri* in Tokyo Bay, Japanese officials sign the Instrument of Surrender. World War II is finally over.

JULY 17–AUGUST 2 Germany

The Potsdam Conference takes place. The "Big Three"—U.S. President Harry Truman, Soviet leader Joseph Stalin, and British Prime Minister Clement Attlee (who has defeated Churchill in a general election on July 5)—meet to discuss postwar policy. Japan is informed that continued resistance will lead to the "utter devastation of the Japanese homeland." This is a veiled reference to the use of atomic weapons.

AUGUST 6 Japan

The B-29 Superfortress *Enola Gay* drops an atomic bomb on the Japanese city of Hiroshima, killing 70,000 and injuring the same number.

EYEWITNESS: Dr. Michihiko Hachiya, Hiroshima, 1945

"Suddenly, a strong flash of light startled me—and then another. So well does one recall little things that I remember vividly how a stone lantern in the garden became brilliantly lit and I debated whether this light was caused by a magnesium flare or sparks from a passing trolley. All over the right side of my body I was cut and bleeding."

Manchuria – a region of northeast China.

Glossary

amphibious assault: an attack by soldiers who land from the sea

appeasement: avoiding conflict by giving in to someone's demands

"buffer state": a country between two enemy states

Chindit: a British soldier who fought behind Japanese lines in Burma

civil war: a war between two opposing groups of citizens of the same country

commandos: special forces soldiers

convoy: a number of ships or vehicles traveling together

corps: a military unit made up of several divisions

counterattack: an attack by a defending force

destroyer: a small, fast warship

division: an army unit made up of 15,000 to 20,000 soldiers

evacuation: the removal of people from a dangerous area

expeditionary force: an army sent to serve abroad

extermination: the murder of an entire people

fascist: a supporter of a strongly nationalistic and militaristic political party

garrison: a military post

ghetto: part of a city where Jews were forced to live

hemorrhage: the bursting of a blood vessel

liberate: to set free

Manchuria: a region of northeast China

marine: a soldier based on a ship who fights on land

morale: the emotional well-being of people

occupation: military control of part of a country by forces from another

panzer: German word for a tank

paratrooper: a soldier who jumps from an aircraft with a parachute

partisan: a soldier who fights behind enemy lines

pocket battleship: a powerful warship smaller than a battleship

rebel: someone who fights against a government or leader

Reichstag: the German parliament

reservists: part of an army called on to fight in an emergency

retaliation: revenge for a previous event

sabotage: destruction of an enemy's property

strategic: something that is useful in achieving a long-term goal

strategy: a long-term plan of action

surrender: to stop fighting and give in to the enemy

U-boat: a German submarine

ultimatum: a demand made by one country on another

uprising: a revolt against a ruler

warlord: a military commander who has political power over a region

"Wolf Pack": a group of 15 to 20 German U-boats

Further resources

BOOKS ABOUT WORLD WAR II

World War II (DK Eyewitness Books) by Simon Adams, DK Children, 2007

V Is for Victory: America Remembers World War II by Kathleen Krull, Knopf Books for Young Readers, 2002

World War II (First Book) by Tom McGowen, Franklin Watts, 1993

Key Battles of World War II (20th Century Perspectives) by Fiona Reynoldson, Heinemann, 2001

World War II in the Pacific (U.S. Wars) by R. Conrad Stein, Enslow Publishers, 2002

Generals of World War II by Mike Taylor, ABDO & Daughters, 1998

USEFUL WEBSITES

www.worldwar-2.net/

www.euronet.nl/users/wilfried/ww2/ww2.htm

www.spartacus.schoolnet.co.uk/2WW.htm

www.eyewitnesstohistory.com/w2frm.htm

www.ibiblio.org/hyperwar/

www.teacheroz.com/wwii.htm

Index